P
MAP®
for the
Grieving Heart

BARBOUR
PUBLISHING

Print ISBN 978-1-63609-306-2

Published by Barbour Publishing, Inc., 1810 Barbour Drive, Uhrichsville, Ohio 44683, www.barbourbooks.com

Our mission is to inspire the world with the life-changing message of the Bible.

Printed in China.

A Comforting Prayer Map for Your Grieving Heart...

Get ready to experience the power of prayer more fully in your life with this creative journal...where every colorful page will guide you to create your very own prayer map— as you write out specific thoughts, ideas, and lists, which you can follow (from start to finish)—as you talk to God. (Be sure to record the date on each one of your prayer maps so you can look back over time and see how God has continued to bring comfort and healing into your life!)

The Prayer Map for the Grieving Heart will not only encourage you to spend time talking with God about the loss that weighs heavy upon your heart...it will also help you build a healthy spiritual habit of continual prayer for life!

Date:

Dear Heavenly Father,

Today, I am really missing. . .

I feel. . .

I need. . .

I am grateful for people and things that bring me comfort, like. . .

....
....
....
....
....

I am thankful for memories, like. . .

....
....
....
....

Other things that I need to share with You, God. . .

....
....
....
....
....

Amen. Thank You, Father, for hearing my prayers.

"Blessed are those who mourn,
for they will be comforted."
MATTHEW 5:4 NIV

Date:

Dear Heavenly Father,...
....
....
....
....

Today, I am really missing. . .
....
....
....
....
....
....
....
....
....
....

I feel. . .
....
....
....
....
....
....
....
....

I need. . .
....
....
....
....
....

I am grateful for people and things that bring me comfort, like. . .

....

....

....

....

....

I am thankful for memories, like. . .

....

....

....

....

Other things that I need to share with You, God. . .

....

....

....

....

....

Amen. Thank You, Father, for hearing my prayers.

This is my comfort in my affliction,
for Your word has given me life.
PSALM 119:50 NKJV

Date:

Dear Heavenly Father,

Today, I am really missing...

I feel...

I need...

I am grateful for people and things that bring me comfort, like. . .

....

....

....

....

....

I am thankful for memories, like. . .

....

....

....

....

Other things that I need to share with You, God. . .

....

....

....

....

....

Amen. Thank You, Father, for hearing my prayers.

*And we know that in all things God
works for the good of those who love him,
who have been called according to his purpose.*
ROMANS 8:28 NIV

Date:

Dear Heavenly Father, ...
....
....
....
....

Today, I am really missing. . .
....
....
....
....
....
....
....
....
....
....
....

I feel. . .
....
....
....
....
....
....
....
....
....

I need. . .
....
....
....
....

I am grateful for people and things that bring me comfort, like...

....
....
....
....
....

I am thankful for memories, like...

....
....
....
....

Other things that I need to share with You, God...

....
....
....
....
....

Amen. Thank You, Father, for hearing my prayers.

When the righteous cry for help, the LORD hears and delivers them out of all their troubles. The LORD is near to the brokenhearted and saves the crushed in spirit.
PSALM 34:17–18 ESV

Date: ....

Dear Heavenly Father, ...
....
....
....
....

Today, I am really missing...
....
....
....
....
....
....
....
....
....
....
....

I feel...
....
....
....
....
....
....
....
....
....
....
....
....

I need...
....
....
....
....

I am grateful for people and things that bring me comfort, like. . .

....

....

....

....

....

I am thankful for memories, like. . .

....

....

....

....

Other things that I need to share with You, God. . .

....

....

....

....

....

Amen. Thank You, Father, for hearing my prayers.

Be gracious to me, O LORD, for I am frail.
PSALM 6:2 NASB

Date:

Dear Heavenly Father,

Today, I am really missing. . .

I feel. . .

I need. . .

I am grateful for people and things that bring me comfort, like. . .

....

....

....

....

....

I am thankful for memories, like. . .

....

....

....

....

Other things that I need to share with You, God. . .

....

....

....

....

....

Amen. Thank You, Father, for hearing my prayers.

"Be strong and courageous, do not be afraid or in dread of them, for the LORD your God is the One who is going with you. He will not desert you or abandon you."
DEUTERONOMY 31:6 NASB

Date:

Dear Heavenly Father, ...
....
....
....
....

Today, I am really missing...
....
....
....
....
....
....
....
....
....
....
....

I feel...
....
....
....
....
....
....
....

I need...
....
....
....
....

I am grateful for people and things that bring me comfort, like. . .

....

....

....

....

....

I am thankful for memories, like. . .

....

....

....

....

Other things that I need to share with You, God. . .

....

....

....

....

....

Amen. Thank You, Father, for hearing my prayers.

May our Lord Jesus Christ himself and God our Father, who loved us and by his grace gave us eternal encouragement and good hope, encourage your hearts and strengthen you in every good deed and word.
2 THESSALONIANS 2:16–17 NIV

Date:

Dear Heavenly Father, ...
....
....
....
....

Today, I am really missing. . .
....
....
....
....
....
....
....
....
....

I feel. . .
....
....
....
....
....
....
....
....

I need. . .
....
....
....
....

I am grateful for people and things that bring me comfort, like. . .

....

....

....

....

I am thankful for memories, like. . .

....

....

....

....

Other things that I need to share with You, God. . .

....

....

....

....

Amen. Thank You, Father, for hearing my prayers.

Humble yourselves, therefore, under God's mighty hand, that he may lift you up in due time. Cast all your anxiety on him because he cares for you.
1 PETER 5:6–7 NIV

Date:

Dear Heavenly Father, ...
....
....
....
....

Today, I am really missing. . .
....
....
....
....
....
....
....
....

I feel. . .
....
....
....
....
....
....
....

I need. . .
....
....
....
....

I am grateful for people and things that bring me comfort, like. . .

....

....

....

....

....

I am thankful for memories, like. . .

....

....

....

....

Other things that I need to share with You, God. . .

....

....

....

....

....

Amen. Thank You, Father, for hearing my prayers.

For Christ also suffered once for sins, the righteous for the unrighteous, that he might bring us to God, being put to death in the flesh but made alive in the spirit.
1 PETER 3:18 ESV

Date:

Dear Heavenly Father,

Today, I am really missing. . .

I feel. . .

I need. . .

I am grateful for people and things that bring me comfort, like. . .

....

....

....

....

....

I am thankful for memories, like. . .

....

....

....

....

Other things that I need to share with You, God. . .

....

....

....

....

....

Amen. Thank You, Father, for hearing my prayers.

For no one is cast off by the Lord forever. Though he brings grief, he will show compassion, so great is his unfailing love. For he does not willingly bring affliction or grief to anyone.
LAMENTATIONS 3:31–33 NIV

Date:

Dear Heavenly Father,

Today, I am really missing...

I feel...

I need...

I am grateful for people and things that bring me comfort, like. . .

....
....
....
....
....

I am thankful for memories, like. . .

....
....
....
....

Other things that I need to share with You, God. . .

....
....
....
....
....

Amen. Thank You, Father, for hearing my prayers.

"I will not leave you as orphans; I will come to you."
JOHN 14:18 NIV

Date:

Dear Heavenly Father, ...
....
....
....
....

Today, I am really missing. . .
....
....
....
....
....
....
....
....
....
....

I feel. . .
....
....
....
....
....
....
....
....
....

I need. . .
....
....
....
....

I am grateful for people and things that bring me comfort, like. . .

....

....

....

....

....

I am thankful for memories, like. . .

....

....

....

....

Other things that I need to share with You, God. . .

....

....

....

....

....

Amen. Thank You, Father, for hearing my prayers.

Even though I walk through the darkest valley,
I will fear no evil, for you are with me;
your rod and your staff, they comfort me.
PSALM 23:4 NIV

Date:

Dear Heavenly Father,..

....

....

....

....

Today, I am really missing. . .

....

....

....

....

....

....

....

....

....

....

I feel. . .

....

....

....

....

....

....

....

....

I need. . .

....

....

....

....

I am grateful for people and things that bring me comfort, like. . .

....

....

....

....

....

I am thankful for memories, like. . .

....

....

....

....

Other things that I need to share with You, God. . .

....

....

....

....

....

Amen. Thank You, Father, for hearing my prayers.

" 'He will wipe every tear from their eyes. There will be no more death' or mourning or crying or pain, for the old order of things has passed away."

REVELATION 21:4 NIV

Date:

Dear Heavenly Father, ...
....
....
....
....

Today, I am really missing. . .
....
....
....
....
....
....
....
....

I feel. . .
....
....
....
....
....
....
....
....

I need. . .
....
....
....
....

I am grateful for people and things that bring me comfort, like...

....

....

....

....

....

I am thankful for memories, like...

....

....

....

....

Other things that I need to share with You, God...

....

....

....

....

Amen. Thank You, Father, for hearing my prayers.

" 'I will give you a new heart and put a new spirit in you; I will remove from you your heart of stone and give you a heart of flesh.' "
EZEKIEL 36:26 NIV

Date:

Dear Heavenly Father, ...
....
....
....
....

Today, I am really missing...
....
....
....
....
....
....
....
....
....
....
....
....

I feel...
....
....
....
....
....
....
....
....
....

I need...
....
....
....
....

I am grateful for people and things that bring me comfort, like. . .

....

....

....

....

I am thankful for memories, like. . .

....

....

....

....

Other things that I need to share with You, God. . .

....

....

....

....

Amen. Thank You, Father, for hearing my prayers.

"Call to me and I will answer you, and will tell you great and hidden things that you have not known."
JEREMIAH 33:3 ESV

Date:

Dear Heavenly Father, ...
....
....
....
....

Today, I am really missing. . .
....
....
....
....
....
....
....
....
....
....
....

I feel. . .
....
....
....
....
....
....
....
....
....

I need. . .
....
....
....
....

I am grateful for people and things that bring me comfort, like. . .

....
....
....
....
....

I am thankful for memories, like. . .

....
....
....
....

Other things that I need to share with You, God. . .

....
....
....
....
....

Amen. Thank You, Father, for hearing my prayers.

*Precious in the sight of the Lord is
the death of his faithful servants.*
Psalm 116:15 niv

Date:

Dear Heavenly Father, ...
....
....
....
....

Today, I am really missing. . .
....
....
....
....
....
....
....
....
....
....
....

I feel. . .
....
....
....
....
....
....
....
....
....

I need. . .
....
....
....
....

I am grateful for people and things that bring me comfort, like. . .

....
....
....
....
....

I am thankful for memories, like. . .

....
....
....
....

Other things that I need to share with You, God. . .

....
....
....
....

Amen. Thank You, Father, for hearing my prayers.

Forgetting what is behind and straining toward what is ahead, I press on toward the goal to win the prize for which God has called me heavenward in Christ Jesus.
PHILIPPIANS 3:13–14 NIV

Date:

Dear Heavenly Father, ...
....
....
....
....

Today, I am really missing. . .
....
....
....
....
....
....
....
....
....
....

I feel. . .
....
....
....
....
....
....
....
....

I need. . .
....
....
....
....

I am grateful for people and things that bring me comfort, like. . .

....

....

....

....

....

I am thankful for memories, like. . .

....

....

....

....

Other things that I need to share with You, God. . .

....

....

....

....

Amen. Thank You, Father, for hearing my prayers.

"The LORD your God is with you, the Mighty Warrior who saves. He will take great delight in you; in his love he will no longer rebuke you, but will rejoice over you with singing."
ZEPHANIAH 3:17 NIV

Date: ....

Dear Heavenly Father, ...
....
....
....
....

Today, I am really missing...
....
....
....
....
....
....
....
....

I feel...
....
....
....
....
....
....
....
....
....

I need...
....
....
....
....

I am grateful for people and things that bring me comfort, like. . .

....
....
....
....
....

I am thankful for memories, like. . .

....
....
....
....

Other things that I need to share with You, God. . .

....
....
....
....
....

Amen. Thank You, Father, for hearing my prayers.

Do not conform to the pattern of this world, but be transformed by the renewing of your mind. Then you will be able to test and approve what God's will is—his good, pleasing and perfect will.
ROMANS 12:2 NIV

Date:

Dear Heavenly Father, ...
....
....
....
....

Today, I am really missing. . .
....
....
....
....
....
....
....
....
....

I feel. . .
....
....
....
....
....
....
....
....

I need. . .
....
....
....
....

I am grateful for people and things that bring me comfort, like. . .

....
....
....
....
....

I am thankful for memories, like. . .

....
....
....
....

Other things that I need to share with You, God. . .

....
....
....
....
....

Amen. Thank You, Father, for hearing my prayers.

"Even to your old age and gray hairs I am he,
I am he who will sustain you. I have made you and I
will sustain you and I will rescue you."
ISAIAH 46:4 NIV

Date:

Dear Heavenly Father, ...
....
....
....
....

Today, I am really missing. . .
....
....
....
....
....
....
....
....
....
....

I feel. . .
....
....
....
....
....
....
....
....
....

I need. . .
....
....
....
....

I am grateful for people and things that bring me comfort, like. . .

....

....

....

....

....

I am thankful for memories, like. . .

....

....

....

....

Other things that I need to share with You, God. . .

....

....

....

....

....

Amen. Thank You, Father, for hearing my prayers.

Being confident of this very thing, that He who has begun a good work in you will complete it until the day of Jesus Christ.
PHILIPPIANS 1:6 NKJV

Date:

Dear Heavenly Father, ...
....
....
....
....

Today, I am really missing. . .
....
....
....
....
....
....
....
....
....
....
....

I feel. . .
....
....
....
....
....
....
....
....
....

I need. . .
....
....
....
....

I am grateful for people and things that bring me comfort, like. . .

....

....

....

....

....

I am thankful for memories, like. . .

....

....

....

....

Other things that I need to share with You, God. . .

....

....

....

....

....

Amen. Thank You, Father, for hearing my prayers.

"Ask, and it will be given to you; seek, and you will find; knock, and it will be opened to you."
MATTHEW 7:7 NKJV

Date:

Dear Heavenly Father,
....
....
....
....
....

Today, I am really missing...
....
....
....
....
....
....
....
....
....

I feel...
....
....
....
....
....
....
....

I need...
....
....
....
....
....

I am grateful for people and things that bring me comfort, like. . .

....

....

....

....

I am thankful for memories, like. . .

....

....

....

....

Other things that I need to share with You, God. . .

....

....

....

....

....

Amen. Thank You, Father, for hearing my prayers.

Why, my soul, are you downcast? Why so disturbed within me? Put your hope in God, for I will yet praise him, my Savior and my God.
PSALM 42:11 NIV

Date:

Dear Heavenly Father, ...
....
....
....
....

Today, I am really missing. . .
....
....
....
....
....
....
....
....
....

I feel. . .
....
....
....
....
....
....
....
....

I need. . .
....
....
....
....

I am grateful for people and things that bring me comfort, like. . .

....
....
....
....
....

I am thankful for memories, like. . .

....
....
....
....

Other things that I need to share with You, God. . .

....
....
....
....
....

Amen. Thank You, Father, for hearing my prayers.

He heals the brokenhearted and binds up their wounds.
PSALM 147:3 NIV

Date:

Dear Heavenly Father,

Today, I am really missing. . .

I feel. . .

I need. . .

I am grateful for people and things that bring me comfort, like. . .

....

....

....

....

....

I am thankful for memories, like. . .

....

....

....

....

Other things that I need to share with You, God. . .

....

....

....

....

....

Amen. Thank You, Father, for hearing my prayers.

"But as for me and my household, we will serve the LORD."
Joshua 24:15 NIV

Date:

Dear Heavenly Father, ...
....
....
....
....

Today, I am really missing. . .
....
....
....
....
....
....
....
....
....

I feel. . .
....
....
....
....
....
....
....
....

I need. . .
....
....
....
....

I am grateful for people and things that bring me comfort, like. . .

I am thankful for memories, like. . .

Other things that I need to share with You, God. . .

Amen. Thank You, Father, for hearing my prayers.

I will instruct you and teach you in the way you should go;
I will counsel you with my loving eye on you.
PSALM 32:8 NIV

Date:

Dear Heavenly Father, ...
....
....
....
....

Today, I am really missing. . .
....
....
....
....
....
....
....
....
....

I feel. . .
....
....
....
....
....
....
....

I need. . .
....
....
....
....

I am grateful for people and things that bring me comfort, like. . .

....

....

....

....

....

I am thankful for memories, like. . .

....

....

....

....

Other things that I need to share with You, God. . .

....

....

....

....

Amen. Thank You, Father, for hearing my prayers.

And we know that in all things God works for the good of those who love him, who have been called according to his purpose.
ROMANS 8:28 NIV

Date:

Dear Heavenly Father, ...
....
....
....
....

Today, I am really missing. . .
....
....
....
....
....
....
....
....
....
....
....

I feel. . .
....
....
....
....
....
....
....
....
....
....

I need. . .
....
....
....
....

I am grateful for people and things that bring me comfort, like. . .

....

....

....

....

....

I am thankful for memories, like. . .

....

....

....

....

Other things that I need to share with You, God. . .

....

....

....

....

....

Amen. Thank You, Father, for hearing my prayers.

Wait for the LORD; be strong and
take heart and wait on the LORD.
PSALM 27:14 NIV

Date:

Dear Heavenly Father, ...
....
....
....
....

Today, I am really missing. . .
....
....
....
....
....
....
....
....
....
....
....

I feel. . .
....
....
....
....
....
....
....
....

I need. . .
....
....
....
....

I am grateful for people and things that bring me comfort, like. . .

....
....
....
....
....

I am thankful for memories, like. . .

....
....
....
....

Other things that I need to share with You, God. . .

....
....
....
....
....

Amen. Thank You, Father, for hearing my prayers.

The LORD is my rock, my fortress and my deliverer;
my God is my rock, in whom I take refuge, my shield
and the horn of my salvation, my stronghold.
PSALM 18:2 NIV

Date:

Dear Heavenly Father, ...
....
....
....
....

Today, I am really missing. . .
....
....
....
....
....
....
....
....
....
....
....

I feel. . .
....
....
....
....
....
....
....
....
....

I need. . .
....
....
....
....

I am grateful for people and things that bring me comfort, like. . .

....

....

....

....

....

I am thankful for memories, like. . .

....

....

....

....

Other things that I need to share with You, God. . .

....

....

....

....

Amen. Thank You, Father, for hearing my prayers.

To every thing there is a season, and a time to every purpose under the heaven: a time to be born, and a time to die. . .a time to weep, and a time to laugh; a time to mourn, and a time to dance.
ECCLESIASTES 3:1–2, 4 KJV

Date:

Dear Heavenly Father,
....
....
....
....
....

Today, I am really missing. . .
....
....
....
....
....
....
....
....
....
....
....

I feel. . .
....
....
....
....
....
....
....
....
....

I need. . .
....
....
....
....
....

I am grateful for people and things that bring me comfort, like. . .

....

....

....

....

....

I am thankful for memories, like. . .

....

....

....

....

Other things that I need to share with You, God. . .

....

....

....

....

....

Amen. Thank You, Father, for hearing my prayers.

"My Father's house has many rooms; if that were not so, would I have told you that I am going there to prepare a place for you?"
JOHN 14:2 NIV

Date:

Dear Heavenly Father,...
....
....
....
....

Today, I am really missing...
....
....
....
....
....
....
....
....
....
....
....

I feel...
....
....
....
....
....
....
....
....

I need...
....
....
....
....

I am grateful for people and things that bring me comfort, like. . .

....
....
....
....
....

I am thankful for memories, like. . .

....
....
....
....

Other things that I need to share with You, God. . .

....
....
....
....

Amen. Thank You, Father, for hearing my prayers.

Brothers and sisters, we do not want you to be uninformed about those who sleep in death, so that you do not grieve like the rest of mankind, who have no hope.
1 THESSALONIANS 4:13 NIV

Date:

Dear Heavenly Father, ...
....
....
....
....

Today, I am really missing. . .
....
....
....
....
....
....
....
....
....

I feel. . .
....
....
....
....
....
....
....
....

I need. . .
....
....
....
....

I am grateful for people and things that bring me comfort, like. . .

....

....

....

....

....

I am thankful for memories, like. . .

....

....

....

....

Other things that I need to share with You, God. . .

....

....

....

....

....

Amen. Thank You, Father, for hearing my prayers.

But thanks be to God! He gives us the victory through our Lord Jesus Christ.
1 CORINTHIANS 15:57 NIV

Date:

Dear Heavenly Father, ...
....
....
....
....

Today, I am really missing. . .
....
....
....
....
....
....
....
....
....
....

I feel. . .
....
....
....
....
....
....
....
....
....

I need. . .
....
....
....
....

I am grateful for people and things that bring me comfort, like. . .

I am thankful for memories, like. . .

Other things that I need to share with You, God. . .

Amen. Thank You, Father, for hearing my prayers.

"Then shall your light break forth like the dawn, and your healing shall spring up speedily; your righteousness shall go before you; the glory of the Lord shall be your rear guard."
ISAIAH 58:8 ESV

Date:

Dear Heavenly Father,..
....
....
....
....

Today, I am really missing. . .
....
....
....
....
....
....
....
....
....

I feel. . .
....
....
....
....
....
....
....
....
....

I need. . .
....
....
....
....

I am grateful for people and things that bring me comfort, like. . .

....

....

....

....

....

I am thankful for memories, like. . .

....

....

....

....

Other things that I need to share with You, God. . .

....

....

....

....

....

Amen. Thank You, Father, for hearing my prayers.

You will keep in perfect peace those whose minds are steadfast, because they trust in you.
ISAIAH 26:3 NIV

Date:

Dear Heavenly Father,

Today, I am really missing. . .

I feel. . .

I need. . .

I am grateful for people and things that bring me comfort, like. . .

....

....

....

....

....

I am thankful for memories, like. . .

....

....

....

....

Other things that I need to share with You, God. . .

....

....

....

....

....

Amen. Thank You, Father, for hearing my prayers.

The LORD is close to the brokenhearted
and saves those who are crushed in spirit.
PSALM 34:18 NIV

Date:

Dear Heavenly Father, ...
....
....
....
....

Today, I am really missing. . .
....
....
....
....
....
....
....
....
....

I feel. . .
....
....
....
....
....
....
....
....

I need. . .
....
....
....
....

I am grateful for people and things that bring me comfort, like. . .

....
....
....
....
....

I am thankful for memories, like. . .

....
....
....
....

Other things that I need to share with You, God. . .

....
....
....
....
....

Amen. Thank You, Father, for hearing my prayers.

Search me, God, and know my heart;
test me and know my anxious thoughts.
PSALM 139:23 NIV

Date:

Dear Heavenly Father,

Today, I am really missing...

I feel...

I need...

I am grateful for people and things that bring me comfort, like. . .

....

....

....

....

....

I am thankful for memories, like. . .

....

....

....

....

Other things that I need to share with You, God. . .

....

....

....

....

Amen. Thank You, Father, for hearing my prayers.

*Yet this I call to mind and therefore I have hope:
Because of the LORD's great love we are not
consumed, for his compassions never fail. They are
new every morning; great is your faithfulness.*
LAMENTATIONS 3:21–23 NIV

Date:

Dear Heavenly Father, ...
....
....
....
....

Today, I am really missing. . .
....
....
....
....
....
....
....
....
....

I feel. . .
....
....
....
....
....
....
....

I need. . .
....
....
....
....

I am grateful for people and things that bring me comfort, like. . .

....

....

....

....

I am thankful for memories, like. . .

....

....

....

....

Other things that I need to share with You, God. . .

....

....

....

....

Amen. Thank You, Father, for hearing my prayers.

*Dear friends, now we are children of God, and
what we will be has not yet been made known.
But we know that when Christ appears, we shall
be like him, for we shall see him as he is.*
1 John 3:2 niv

Date: _____

Dear Heavenly Father, ...
....
....
....
....

Today, I am really missing. . .
....
....
....
....
....
....
....
....

I feel. . .
....
....
....
....
....
....
....
....

I need. . .
....
....
....
....

I am grateful for people and things that bring me comfort, like. . .

....
....
....
....
....

I am thankful for memories, like. . .

....
....
....
....

Other things that I need to share with You, God. . .

....
....
....
....
....

Amen. Thank You, Father, for hearing my prayers.

Surely goodness and mercy shall follow me all the days of my life, and I shall dwell in the house of the LORD forever.
PSALM 23:6 ESV

Date:

Dear Heavenly Father,...
....
....
....
....

Today, I am really missing...
....
....
....
....
....
....
....
....
....
....

I feel...
....
....
....
....
....
....
....
....
....

I need...
....
....
....
....

I am grateful for people and things that bring me comfort, like. . .

....
....
....
....
....

I am thankful for memories, like. . .

....
....
....
....

Other things that I need to share with You, God. . .

....
....
....
....
....

Amen. Thank You, Father, for hearing my prayers.

*"Have I not commanded you? Be strong and courageous.
Do not be afraid; do not be discouraged, for the LORD
your God will be with you wherever you go."*

JOSHUA 1:9 NIV

Date:

Dear Heavenly Father,

Today, I am really missing. . .

I feel. . .

I need. . .

I am grateful for people and things that bring me comfort, like. . .

....

....

....

....

....

I am thankful for memories, like. . .

....

....

....

....

Other things that I need to share with You, God. . .

....

....

....

....

....

Amen. Thank You, Father, for hearing my prayers.

I remember the days of old; I meditate on all that you have done; I ponder the work of your hands.
PSALM 143:5 ESV

Date:

Dear Heavenly Father, ...
....
....
....
....

Today, I am really missing. . .
....
....
....
....
....
....
....

I feel. . .
....
....
....
....
....
....
....
....

I need. . .
....
....
....
....

I am grateful for people and things that bring me comfort, like. . .

....

....

....

....

....

I am thankful for memories, like. . .

....

....

....

....

Other things that I need to share with You, God. . .

....

....

....

....

....

Amen. Thank You, Father, for hearing my prayers.

Let love and faithfulness never leave you; bind them around your neck, write them on the tablet of your heart.
PROVERBS 3:3 NIV

Date: ....

Dear Heavenly Father, ...
....
....
....
....

Today, I am really missing. . .
....
....
....
....
....
....
....
....
....

I feel. . .
....
....
....
....
....
....
....
....
....

I need. . .
....
....
....
....

I am grateful for people and things that bring me comfort, like. . .

....
....
....
....
....

I am thankful for memories, like. . .

....
....
....
....

Other things that I need to share with You, God. . .

....
....
....
....

Amen. Thank You, Father, for hearing my prayers.

"Be still, and know that I am God."
PSALM 46:10 ESV

Date: _____

Dear Heavenly Father, ...
....
....
....
....

Today, I am really missing. . .
....
....
....
....
....
....
....
....
....
....

I feel. . .
....
....
....
....
....
....
....
....

I need. . .
....
....
....
....

I am grateful for people and things that bring me comfort, like. . .

....

....

....

....

....

I am thankful for memories, like. . .

....

....

....

....

Other things that I need to share with You, God. . .

....

....

....

....

....

Amen. Thank You, Father, for hearing my prayers.

*Whom have I in heaven but you? And there
is nothing on earth that I desire besides you.
My flesh and my heart may fail, but God is the
strength of my heart and my portion forever.*
PSALM 73:25–26 ESV

Date:

Dear Heavenly Father, ...
....
....
....
....

Today, I am really missing. . .
....
....
....
....
....
....
....
....
....
....

I feel . . .
....
....
....
....
....
....
....
....
....

I need . . .
....
....
....
....

I am grateful for people and things that bring me comfort, like. . .

....

....

....

....

....

I am thankful for memories, like. . .

....

....

....

....

Other things that I need to share with You, God. . .

....

....

....

....

....

Amen. Thank You, Father, for hearing my prayers.

I think it is right to refresh your memory
as long as I live in the tent of this body.
2 PETER 1:13 NIV

Date:

Dear Heavenly Father,..
....
....
....
....

Today, I am really missing. . .
....
....
....
....
....
....
....
....
....
....

I feel. . .
....
....
....
....
....
....
....
....

I need. . .
....
....
....
....

I am grateful for people and things that bring me comfort, like. . .

_____

_____

_____

_____

_____

I am thankful for memories, like. . .

_____

_____

_____

_____

Other things that I need to share with You, God. . .

_____

_____

_____

_____

_____

Amen. Thank You, Father, for hearing my prayers.

"Do not let your hearts be troubled.
You believe in God; believe also in me."
JOHN 14:1 NIV

Date:

Dear Heavenly Father,..
....
....
....
....

Today, I am really missing...
....
....
....
....
....
....
....
....
....
....

I feel...
....
....
....
....
....
....
....

I need...
....
....
....
....

I am grateful for people and things that bring me comfort, like. . .

....

....

....

....

....

I am thankful for memories, like. . .

....

....

....

....

Other things that I need to share with You, God. . .

....

....

....

....

....

Amen. Thank You, Father, for hearing my prayers.

"Because he holds fast to me in love, I will deliver him;
I will protect him, because he knows my name."
PSALM 91:14 ESV

Date:

Dear Heavenly Father, ...
....
....
....
....

Today, I am really missing. . .
....
....
....
....
....
....
....
....
....
....

I feel. . .
....
....
....
....
....
....
....
....

I need. . .
....
....
....
....

I am grateful for people and things that bring me comfort, like. . .

....

....

....

....

....

I am thankful for memories, like. . .

....

....

....

....

Other things that I need to share with You, God. . .

....

....

....

....

Amen. Thank You, Father, for hearing my prayers.

But we have this treasure in earthen containers, so that the extraordinary greatness of the power will be of God and not from ourselves; we are afflicted in every way, but not crushed; perplexed, but not despairing.
2 CORINTHIANS 4:7–8 NASB

Date:

Dear Heavenly Father, ...
....
....
....
....

Today, I am really missing. . .
....
....
....
....
....
....
....
....

I feel. . .
....
....
....
....
....
....
....
....

I need. . .
....
....
....
....

I am grateful for people and things that bring me comfort, like. . .

....

....

....

....

....

I am thankful for memories, like. . .

....

....

....

....

Other things that I need to share with You, God. . .

....

....

....

....

....

Amen. Thank You, Father, for hearing my prayers.

For I consider that the sufferings of this present time are not worth comparing with the glory that is to be revealed to us.
ROMANS 8:18 ESV

Date:

Dear Heavenly Father, ...
....
....
....
....

Today, I am really missing. . .
....
....
....
....
....
....
....
....
....

I feel. . .
....
....
....
....
....
....
....

I need. . .
....
....
....
....

I am grateful for people and things that bring me comfort, like. . .

....
....
....
....
....

I am thankful for memories, like. . .

....
....
....
....

Other things that I need to share with You, God. . .

....
....
....
....
....

Amen. Thank You, Father, for hearing my prayers.

Be merciful to me, Lord, for I am in distress; my eyes grow weak with sorrow, my soul and body with grief.
Psalm 31:9 niv

Dear Heavenly Father,...
....
....
....
....

Today, I am really missing. . .
....
....
....
....
....
....
....
....
....

I feel. . .
....
....
....
....
....
....
....
....
....
....

I need. . .
....
....
....
....

I am grateful for people and things that bring me comfort, like. . .

....
....
....
....
....

I am thankful for memories, like. . .

....
....
....
....

Other things that I need to share with You, God. . .

....
....
....
....
....

Amen. Thank You, Father, for hearing my prayers.

*So we fix our eyes not on what is seen,
but on what is unseen, since what is seen is
temporary, but what is unseen is eternal.*
2 CORINTHIANS 4:18 NIV

Date:

Dear Heavenly Father, ...
....
....
....
....

Today, I am really missing. . .
....
....
....
....
....
....
....
....
....
....

I feel. . .
....
....
....
....
....
....
....
....
....

I need. . .
....
....
....
....

I am grateful for people and things that bring me comfort, like. . .

....
....
....
....
....

I am thankful for memories, like. . .

....
....
....
....

Other things that I need to share with You, God. . .

....
....
....
....

Amen. Thank You, Father, for hearing my prayers.

For though I am absent in body, yet I am with you in spirit, rejoicing to see your good order and the firmness of your faith in Christ.
COLOSSIANS 2:5 ESV

Date:

Dear Heavenly Father,
....
....
....
....

Today, I am really missing. . .
....
....
....
....
....
....
....
....
....

I feel. . .
....
....
....
....
....
....
....
....

I need. . .
....
....
....
....

I am grateful for people and things that bring me comfort, like. . .

....

....

....

....

....

I am thankful for memories, like. . .

....

....

....

....

Other things that I need to share with You, God. . .

....

....

....

....

....

Amen. Thank You, Father, for hearing my prayers.

My comfort in my suffering is this:
Your promise preserves my life.
PSALM 119:50 NIV

Date: ....

Dear Heavenly Father, ...
....
....
....
....

Today, I am really missing. . .
....
....
....
....
....
....
....
....
....

I feel. . .
....
....
....
....
....
....
....
....
....

I need. . .
....
....
....
....

I am grateful for people and things that bring me comfort, like. . .

....

....

....

....

....

I am thankful for memories, like. . .

....

....

....

....

Other things that I need to share with You, God. . .

....

....

....

....

Amen. Thank You, Father, for hearing my prayers.

Bear one another's burdens,
and thereby fulfill the law of Christ.
GALATIANS 6:2 NASB

Date:

Dear Heavenly Father, ...
....
....
....
....

Today, I am really missing. . .
....
....
....
....
....
....
....
....

I feel. . .
....
....
....
....
....
....
....
....

I need. . .
....
....
....
....

I am grateful for people and things that bring me comfort, like. . .

....
....
....
....
....

I am thankful for memories, like. . .

....
....
....
....

Other things that I need to share with You, God. . .

....
....
....
....
....

Amen. Thank You, Father, for hearing my prayers.

In peace I will lie down and sleep, for you alone, LORD, make me dwell in safety.
PSALM 4:8 NIV

Date:

Dear Heavenly Father,

Today, I am really missing. . .

I feel. . .

I need. . .

I am grateful for people and things that bring me comfort, like. . .

....
....
....
....
....

I am thankful for memories, like. . .

....
....
....
....

Other things that I need to share with You, God. . .

....
....
....
....

Amen. Thank You, Father, for hearing my prayers.

For the LORD your God is a merciful God; he will not abandon or destroy you or forget the covenant with your ancestors, which he confirmed to them by oath.
DEUTERONOMY 4:31 NIV

Date:

Dear Heavenly Father, ...
....
....
....
....

Today, I am really missing. . .
....
....
....
....
....
....
....
....
....
....

I feel. . .
....
....
....
....
....
....
....
....
....
....

I need. . .
....
....
....
....

I am grateful for people and things that bring me comfort, like. . .

....

....

....

....

....

I am thankful for memories, like. . .

....

....

....

....

Other things that I need to share with You, God. . .

....

....

....

....

....

Amen. Thank You, Father, for hearing my prayers.

Now to Him who is able to do far more abundantly beyond all that we ask or think, according to the power that works within us, to Him be the glory in the church and in Christ Jesus to all generations forever and ever.
EPHESIANS 3:20–21 NASB

Date: ....

Dear Heavenly Father, ...
....
....
....
....

Today, I am really missing. . .
....
....
....
....
....
....
....
....
....

I feel. . .
....
....
....
....
....
....
....
....
....

I need. . .
....
....
....
....

I am grateful for people and things that bring me comfort, like. . .

....
....
....
....
....

I am thankful for memories, like. . .

....
....
....
....

Other things that I need to share with You, God. . .

....
....
....
....
....

Amen. Thank You, Father, for hearing my prayers.

No one has ever seen God; but if we love one another,
God lives in us and his love is made complete in us.
1 JOHN 4:12 NIV

Date:

Dear Heavenly Father,

_____

_____

_____

_____

Today, I am really missing. . .

_____

_____

_____

_____

_____

_____

_____

_____

_____

I feel. . .

_____

_____

_____

_____

_____

_____

_____

_____

_____

I need. . .

_____

_____

_____

_____

I am grateful for people and things that bring me comfort, like. . .

....

....

....

....

....

I am thankful for memories, like. . .

....

....

....

....

Other things that I need to share with You, God. . .

....

....

....

....

....

Amen. Thank You, Father, for hearing my prayers.

*"In all things I have shown you that by working hard
in this way we must help the weak and remember
the words of the Lord Jesus, how he himself said,
'It is more blessed to give than to receive.' "*
ACTS 20:35 ESV

Date:

Dear Heavenly Father,...
....
....
....
....

Today, I am really missing. . .
....
....
....
....
....
....
....
....
....
....

I feel. . .
....
....
....
....
....
....
....
....
....

I need. . .
....
....
....
....

I am grateful for people and things that bring me comfort, like. . .

....

....

....

....

....

I am thankful for memories, like. . .

....

....

....

....

Other things that I need to share with You, God. . .

....

....

....

....

Amen. Thank You, Father, for hearing my prayers.

*Listen, I tell you a mystery: We will not
all sleep, but we will all be changed.*
1 CORINTHIANS 15:51 NIV

Date:

Dear Heavenly Father, ...
....
....
....
....

Today, I am really missing. . .
....
....
....
....
....
....
....
....
....

I feel. . .
....
....
....
....
....
....
....
....
....

I need. . .
....
....
....
....

I am grateful for people and things that bring me comfort, like. . .

....

....

....

....

....

I am thankful for memories, like. . .

....

....

....

....

Other things that I need to share with You, God. . .

....

....

....

....

Amen. Thank You, Father, for hearing my prayers.

For the LORD God is a sun and shield; the LORD bestows favor and honor. No good thing does he withhold from those who walk uprightly.
PSALM 84:11 ESV

Date:

Dear Heavenly Father,..

....

....

....

....

Today, I am really missing...

....

....

....

....

....

....

....

....

I feel...

....

....

....

....

....

....

....

I need...

....

....

....

....

I am grateful for people and things that bring me comfort, like. . .

....

....

....

....

....

I am thankful for memories, like. . .

....

....

....

....

Other things that I need to share with You, God. . .

....

....

....

....

....

Amen. Thank You, Father, for hearing my prayers.

You make known to me the path of life;
you will fill me with joy in your presence,
with eternal pleasures at your right hand.
PSALM 16:11 NIV

Date:

Dear Heavenly Father, ...
....
....
....
....

Today, I am really missing. . .
....
....
....
....
....
....
....
....
....

I feel. . .
....
....
....
....
....
....
....
....
....

I need. . .
....
....
....
....

I am grateful for people and things that bring me comfort, like. . .

_____

_____

_____

_____

_____

I am thankful for memories, like. . .

_____

_____

_____

_____

Other things that I need to share with You, God. . .

_____

_____

_____

_____

Amen. Thank You, Father, for hearing my prayers.

And the redeemed of the LORD will return and come to Zion with joyful shouting and everlasting joy will be on their heads. They will obtain gladness and joy, and sorrow and sighing will flee away.
ISAIAH 51:11 NASB

Date:

Dear Heavenly Father,

_____
_____
_____
_____
_____

Today, I am really missing. . .

_____
_____
_____
_____
_____
_____
_____
_____
_____
_____

I feel. . .

_____
_____
_____
_____
_____
_____
_____
_____
_____

I need. . .

_____
_____
_____
_____

I am grateful for people and things that bring me comfort, like. . .

....
....
....
....
....

I am thankful for memories, like. . .

....
....
....
....

Other things that I need to share with You, God. . .

....
....
....
....

Amen. Thank You, Father, for hearing my prayers.

And above all these put on love, which binds everything together in perfect harmony.
COLOSSIANS 3:14 ESV

Date:

Dear Heavenly Father, ...
....
....
....
....

Today, I am really missing. . .
....
....
....
....
....
....
....
....

I feel. . .
....
....
....
....
....
....
....
....

I need. . .
....
....
....
....

I am grateful for people and things that bring me comfort, like. . .

....

....

....

....

....

I am thankful for memories, like. . .

....

....

....

....

Other things that I need to share with You, God. . .

....

....

....

....

Amen. Thank You, Father, for hearing my prayers.

"Abba, Father," he said, "everything is possible for you. Take this cup from me. Yet not what I will, but what you will."
MARK 14:36 NIV

Date:

Dear Heavenly Father, ...
....
....
....
....

Today, I am really missing. . .
....
....
....
....
....
....
....
....
....
....
....

I feel. . .
....
....
....
....
....
....
....
....

I need. . .
....
....
....
....

I am grateful for people and things that bring me comfort, like. . .

....

....

....

....

....

I am thankful for memories, like. . .

....

....

....

....

Other things that I need to share with You, God. . .

....

....

....

....

Amen. Thank You, Father, for hearing my prayers.

But do not overlook this one fact, beloved, that with the Lord one day is as a thousand years, and a thousand years as one day.
2 PETER 3:8 ESV

Date:

Dear Heavenly Father,...
....
....
....
....

Today, I am really missing. . .
....
....
....
....
....
....
....
....
....

I feel. . .
....
....
....
....
....
....
....
....

I need. . .
....
....
....
....

I am grateful for people and things that bring me comfort, like. . .

I am thankful for memories, like. . .

Other things that I need to share with You, God. . .

Amen. Thank You, Father, for hearing my prayers.

Jesus said to her, "I am the resurrection and the life. The one who believes in me will live, even though they die."
JOHN 11:25 NIV

Date:

Dear Heavenly Father,
....
....
....
....
....

Today, I am really missing. . .
....
....
....
....
....
....
....
....
....
....
....

I feel. . .
....
....
....
....
....
....
....
....
....
....

I need. . .
....
....
....
....

I am grateful for people and things that bring me comfort, like. . .

....

....

....

....

....

I am thankful for memories, like. . .

....

....

....

....

Other things that I need to share with You, God. . .

....

....

....

....

....

Amen. Thank You, Father, for hearing my prayers.

"The eternal God is your refuge, and underneath are the everlasting arms. He will drive out your enemies before you, saying, 'Destroy them!' "
DEUTERONOMY 33:27 NIV

Date:

Dear Heavenly Father, ...
....
....
....
....

Today, I am really missing. . .
....

I feel. . .
....

I need. . .
....

I am grateful for people and things that bring me comfort, like. . .

....

....

....

....

....

I am thankful for memories, like. . .

....

....

....

....

Other things that I need to share with You, God. . .

....

....

....

....

....

Amen. Thank You, Father, for hearing my prayers.

"Truly I tell you, if anyone says to this mountain,
'Go, throw yourself into the sea,' and does not
doubt in their heart but believes that what they
say will happen, it will be done for them."
MARK 11:23 NIV

Date:

Dear Heavenly Father,

Today, I am really missing. . .

I feel. . .

I need. . .

I am grateful for people and things that bring me comfort, like. . .

_____

_____

_____

_____

_____

I am thankful for memories, like. . .

_____

_____

_____

_____

Other things that I need to share with You, God. . .

_____

_____

_____

_____

_____

Amen. Thank You, Father, for hearing my prayers.

"Then you will call on me and come and pray to me, and I will listen to you."
JEREMIAH 29:12 NIV

Date:

Dear Heavenly Father, ...
....
....
....
....

Today, I am really missing. . .
....
....
....
....
....
....
....
....
....

I feel. . .
....
....
....
....
....
....
....
....

I need. . .
....
....
....
....

I am grateful for people and things that bring me comfort, like. . .

....
....
....
....
....

I am thankful for memories, like. . .

....
....
....
....

Other things that I need to share with You, God. . .

....
....
....
....

Amen. Thank You, Father, for hearing my prayers.

"Where, O death, is your victory?
Where, O death, is your sting?"
1 CORINTHIANS 15:55 NIV

Date:

Dear Heavenly Father,
....
....
....
....
....

Today, I am really missing. . .
....
....
....
....
....
....
....
....
....
....

I feel. . .
....
....
....
....
....
....
....
....
....
....

I need. . .
....
....
....
....
....

I am grateful for people and things that bring me comfort, like. . .

....

....

....

....

....

I am thankful for memories, like. . .

....

....

....

....

Other things that I need to share with You, God. . .

....

....

....

....

Amen. Thank You, Father, for hearing my prayers.

My soul is weary with sorrow;
strengthen me according to your word.
PSALM 119:28 NIV

Date:

Dear Heavenly Father,
....
....
....
....
....

Today, I am really missing. . .
....
....
....
....
....
....
....
....

I feel. . .
....
....
....
....
....
....
....
....

I need. . .
....
....
....
....

I am grateful for people and things that bring me comfort, like. . .

....
....
....
....
....

I am thankful for memories, like. . .

....
....
....
....

Other things that I need to share with You, God. . .

....
....
....
....
....

Amen. Thank You, Father, for hearing my prayers.

From the ends of the earth I call to you, I call as my heart grows faint; lead me to the rock that is higher than I.
PSALM 61:2 NIV

Date:

Dear Heavenly Father,..
....
....
....
....

Today, I am really missing. . .
....
....
....
....
....
....
....
....
....

I feel. . .
....
....
....
....
....
....
....

I need. . .
....
....
....
....

I am grateful for people and things that bring me comfort, like. . .

....

....

....

....

....

I am thankful for memories, like. . .

....

....

....

....

Other things that I need to share with You, God. . .

....

....

....

....

....

Amen. Thank You, Father, for hearing my prayers.

We are of good courage and prefer rather to be absent from the body and to be at home with the Lord.
2 CORINTHIANS 5:8 NASB

Date:

Dear Heavenly Father, ...
....
....
....
....

Today, I am really missing. . .
....
....
....
....
....
....
....
....
....
....
....

I feel. . .
....
....
....
....
....
....
....
....
....

I need. . .
....
....
....
....

I am grateful for people and things that bring me comfort, like. . .

....

....

....

....

....

I am thankful for memories, like. . .

....

....

....

....

Other things that I need to share with You, God. . .

....

....

....

....

....

Amen. Thank You, Father, for hearing my prayers.

The LORD is my shepherd, I lack nothing.
PSALM 23:1 NIV

Date:

Dear Heavenly Father, ...
....
....
....
....

Today, I am really missing...
....
....
....
....
....
....
....
....
....
....

I feel...
....
....
....
....
....
....
....
....
....

I need...
....
....
....
....

I am grateful for people and things that bring me comfort, like. . .

....

....

....

....

....

I am thankful for memories, like. . .

....

....

....

....

Other things that I need to share with You, God. . .

....

....

....

....

....

Amen. Thank You, Father, for hearing my prayers.

Be completely humble and gentle; be patient, bearing with one another in love. Make every effort to keep the unity of the Spirit through the bond of peace.
EPHESIANS 4:2–3 NIV

Date:

Dear Heavenly Father,..
....
....
....
....

Today, I am really missing. . .
....
....
....
....
....
....
....
....
....
....

I feel. . .
....
....
....
....
....
....
....
....
....
....

I need. . .
....
....
....
....

I am grateful for people and things that bring me comfort, like. . .

....

....

....

....

I am thankful for memories, like. . .

....

....

....

....

Other things that I need to share with You, God. . .

....

....

....

....

....

Amen. Thank You, Father, for hearing my prayers.

He will cover you with his feathers, and under his wings you will find refuge; his faithfulness will be your shield and rampart.
PSALM 91:4 NIV

Date: _____

Dear Heavenly Father, _____
_____
_____
_____
_____

Today, I am really missing. . .
_____
_____
_____
_____
_____
_____
_____
_____
_____
_____

I feel. . .
_____
_____
_____
_____
_____
_____
_____
_____

I need. . .
_____
_____
_____
_____

I am grateful for people and things that bring me comfort, like. . .

....

....

....

....

....

I am thankful for memories, like. . .

....

....

....

....

Other things that I need to share with You, God. . .

....

....

....

....

Amen. Thank You, Father, for hearing my prayers.

And after you have suffered a little while, the God of all grace, who has called you to his eternal glory in Christ, will himself restore, confirm, strengthen, and establish you.
1 PETER 5:10 ESV

Date:

Dear Heavenly Father, ...
....
....
....
....

Today, I am really missing. . .
....
....
....
....
....
....
....
....
....
....

I feel. . .
....
....
....
....
....
....
....
....

I need. . .
....
....
....
....

I am grateful for people and things that bring me comfort, like. . .

....

....

....

....

....

I am thankful for memories, like. . .

....

....

....

....

Other things that I need to share with You, God. . .

....

....

....

....

Amen. Thank You, Father, for hearing my prayers.

"Praise be to you, LORD, the God of our father Israel, from everlasting to everlasting. Yours, LORD, is the greatness and the power and the glory and the majesty and the splendor, for everything in heaven and earth is yours."
1 CHRONICLES 29:10–11 NIV

Date:

Dear Heavenly Father,

Today, I am really missing. . .

I feel. . .

I need. . .

I am grateful for people and things that bring me comfort, like. . .

....

....

....

....

....

I am thankful for memories, like. . .

....

....

....

....

Other things that I need to share with You, God. . .

....

....

....

....

Amen. Thank You, Father, for hearing my prayers.

We pray this so that the name of our Lord Jesus may be glorified in you, and you in him, according to the grace of our God and the Lord Jesus Christ.
2 THESSALONIANS 1:12 NIV

Date:

Dear Heavenly Father,
....
....
....
....
....

Today, I am really missing. . .
....
....
....
....
....
....
....
....
....
....
....

I feel. . .
....
....
....
....
....
....
....
....
....
....

I need. . .
....
....
....
....

I am grateful for people and things that bring me comfort, like. . .

....

....

....

....

....

I am thankful for memories, like. . .

....

....

....

....

Other things that I need to share with You, God. . .

....

....

....

....

....

Amen. Thank You, Father, for hearing my prayers.

" 'Do not fear, for I am with you; do not be afraid, for I am your God. I will strengthen you, I will also help you, I will also uphold you with My righteous right hand.' "
ISAIAH 41:10 NASB

Date:

Dear Heavenly Father,
....
....
....
....
....

Today, I am really missing. . .
....
....
....
....
....
....
....
....
....
....
....

I feel. . .
....
....
....
....
....
....
....
....
....

I need. . .
....
....
....
....

I am grateful for people and things that bring me comfort, like. . .

....
....
....
....
....

I am thankful for memories, like. . .

....
....
....
....

Other things that I need to share with You, God. . .

....
....
....
....
....

Amen. Thank You, Father, for hearing my prayers.

"Therefore do not worry about tomorrow,
for tomorrow will worry about itself.
Each day has enough trouble of its own."
MATTHEW 6:34 NIV

Date:

Dear Heavenly Father, ...
....
....
....
....

Today, I am really missing. . .
....
....
....
....
....
....
....
....
....
....

I feel. . .
....
....
....
....
....
....
....
....

I need. . .
....
....
....
....

I am grateful for people and things that bring me comfort, like. . .

....
....
....
....
....

I am thankful for memories, like. . .

....
....
....
....

Other things that I need to share with You, God. . .

....
....
....
....
....

Amen. Thank You, Father, for hearing my prayers.

*But we all, with unveiled faces, looking as
in a mirror the glory of the Lord, are being
transformed into the same image from glory
to glory, just as from the Lord, the Spirit.*
2 CORINTHIANS 3:18 NASB

Date: _____

Dear Heavenly Father, ...
....
....
....
....

Today, I am really missing. . .
....
....
....
....
....
....
....
....
....

I feel. . .
....
....
....
....
....
....
....
....
....
....

I need. . .
....
....
....
....

I am grateful for people and things that bring me comfort, like. . .

....

....

....

....

....

I am thankful for memories, like. . .

....

....

....

....

Other things that I need to share with You, God. . .

....

....

....

....

....

Amen. Thank You, Father, for hearing my prayers.

*I believe that I shall look upon the goodness
of the LORD in the land of the living!*
PSALM 27:13 ESV

Date:

Dear Heavenly Father,

Today, I am really missing. . .

I feel. . .

I need. . .

I am grateful for people and things that bring me comfort, like. . .

....

....

....

....

....

I am thankful for memories, like. . .

....

....

....

....

Other things that I need to share with You, God. . .

....

....

....

....

....

Amen. Thank You, Father, for hearing my prayers.

"For God so loved the world, that He gave His only Son, so that everyone who believes in Him will not perish, but have eternal life."

JOHN 3:16 NASB

Discover More Faith Maps
for the Entire Family. . .

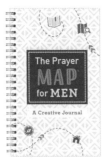  

The Prayer Map for Men
978-1-64352-438-2

The Prayer Map for Women
978-1-68322-557-7

The Prayer Map for Girls
978-1-68322-559-1

The Prayer Map for Boys
978-1-68322-558-4

The Prayer Map for Teens
978-1-68322-556-0

These purposeful prayer journals are a fun and creative way to more fully experience the power of prayer. Each page guides you to write out thoughts, ideas, and lists. . .creating a specific "map" for you to follow as you talk to God. Each map includes a spot to record the date, so you can look back on your prayers and see how God has worked in your life. *The Prayer Map* will not only encourage you to spend time talking with God about the things that matter most. . .it will also help you build a healthy spiritual habit of continual prayer for life!

Spiral Bound / $7.99